MUM,
THE DOG'S DRUNK
AGAIN!

Cardiff Libraries
www.cardiff.gov.uk/libraries

Llyfrgelloedd Caerdydd
www.caerdydd.gov.uk/llyfrgelloedd

This book is dedicated to Carol and Lee

Mum, the Dog's Drunk Again!

by
Gez Walsh

Illustrated by the author

The King's England Press
2004

ISBN 1 872438 95 4

Mum, the Dog's Drunk Again!
is typeset by
Moose Manuscripts
in Arial Rounded MT Bold 14pt and published by

The King's England Press,
Cambertown House, Commercial Road, Goldthorpe,
Rotherham, South Yorkshire, S63 9BL

Printed and bound in Great Britain by:

Antony Rowe Ltd.
Chippenham
Wiltshire

Foreword

If authors were awarded prizes for topping the laughometer scale, then Mr Spot on My Bum Gez Walsh would win hands down. Despite the traditional view of poetry as an out-of-the-ordinary interest, an acquired taste, Potty Poet Gez Walsh has produced some extraordinary books, books for which hundreds of thousands of people have not merely acquired a taste but have gobbled ravenously and demanded more, seven more to be exact. In fact, we have to keep Gez on a tight leash, otherwise we'd be bombarded with a new book every week as, I'm sure everyone who's ever met him knows, this author has a funny story for every occasion.

I'm Debbie, by the way, Gez's editor. Armed with an NVQ in Spots, Bums and Farts, my job is to put lots of red biro on Gez's manuscripts to correct the terrible spelling and make a book from the bizarre poems and stories that pour out of his weird imagination. Once finally translated from Gezspeak into English, I have to ensure that everything can be safely contained within 64 pages of sheer madness which won't frighten your granny or prove harmful to teachers.

If you enjoy *Mum, the Dog's Drunk Again!* spare a thought for the poor editor who's worked day and night on this book. If you don't enjoy it, seek medical advice then contact the author!

Mum, the Dog's Drunk Again!

Dad put out a bowl of beer
To keep slugs off his veg,
But our stupid dog drank it
Then fell into the hedge.

He started to wail,
Which drove us all mad,
Then he ate my trainers
And tried to have sex with Dad.

He barked to next door's dog
That they would be friends forever
Before snuggling up to the cat
Saying, "We want to be together!"

Mum said, "I think he's drunk.
Come on, good boy, Rover."
The dog gave her a soppy grin
Then the stupid mutt fell over.

Next morning when he woke,
With a headache he couldn't bear,
He had a road cone in his kennel
And thought, "How did that get there?"

Cheese of Doom

There's an awful smell in my house,
It's coming from my bedroom.
I don't know what it is
But it smells like the cheese of doom.

Mum says she knows what it is,
It's my socks that reek.
I think she's talking rubbish -
I've only had them on for a week!

Nelly

There was once a woman called Nelly
Who would eat nothing else but jelly.
She didn't give a fig
That she had become so big
And used a wheelbarrow to carry her belly.

Who Weed on the Toilet Seat?

Every night at our house
My Mum and sister will bleat
To my brother, Dad and me:
"Who's weed on the toilet seat?"

They say, "Just lift the seat up!"
And that men and boys don't think.
I don't know why they're blaming me
Because I always wee in the sink!

Our Dinner Lady

Our dinner lady
Is big and fat,
Our dinner lady
Serves food with a splat!
Our dinner lady
Has a nasty rash,
Our dinner lady
Has a moustache.
Our dinner lady
Drinks beer from a can,
She says she's a lady
But we think she's a man.

Pooh Sue

There was a young girl called Sue,
Who worked at the local zoo.
She must've been out of her mind
To stand under an elephant's behind
Because now she's covered in pooh!

The Spider Bath

I'm not going in there,
You're having a laugh:
There's a dirty great spider
Hiding in the bath!
It's got long, skinny legs
That twist and bend;
It must have teeth,
I don't know at which end.
It knows I'm scared;
Look, it can tell.
Well, I'm not having a bath,
I would rather smell!

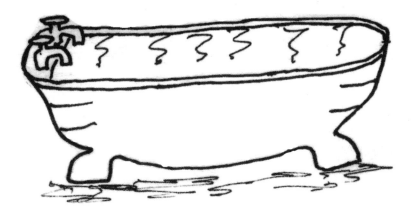

Vindaloo, the Alien-Slayer

The day aliens invaded Ahmed's school
They were scary looking creatures.
They said if they weren't fed straight away
They would eat all the kids and teachers.

Everyone was so frightened,
But Ahmed kept his cool.
On his mobile he phoned his granny -
He knew that she would save his school.

As the school doors swung open
There stood Ahmed's granny with her pot
Which was filled to the top with curry
That could fuel a rocket, it was so hot.

Granny walked up to an alien
And stared in his one, big, bloodshot eye.
She said, "I'm Ahmed's granny,
I guess you're an alien guy.

"I hear that you want feeding.
Well, to get you in the mood,
Get your gnashers round this,
Its good authentic Asian food."

Ahmed's friend, Wayne, grabbed his arm
And whispered, "What is she going to do?"
Ahmed replied, "They're in trouble now,
She's going to feed them her vindaloo!"

As the aliens ate the curry
Their teeth melted to their gums.
They screamed as steam hissed from their ears
And fire roared out of their bums.

Granny shouted out to the school,
"Oh no, blinking heck!
If you don't want to be covered with alien bits
I suggest you all hit the deck."

As the school dived to the floor
The aliens blew, like granny had said:
There were bits of alien everywhere
And an eyeball bounced off a teacher's head.

As granny picked up her curry pot
She could hear the caretaker bawl:
"Look at the mess that you've made,
Who is going to clean up this hall?"

Granny said, "Not me son,
I have done what I came here to do,
And if you don't show more respect
I'll force-feed you my vindaloo."

So if there are any aliens reading this
Then listen to what I have to say:
If you are planning to invade Earth,
Ahmed's granny is just a phone call away!

Bad Teeth

There was an old man from Neath
Who had very bad yellow teeth,
But things soon improved
When he had them removed
By a very nice dentist called Keith.

Hedgehog Pies

Alfred said, "To these pies I'm sticking,
I think they're totally finger-licking."
But what he didn't realise
Was that they were hedgehog pies;
He thought they were made from chicken.

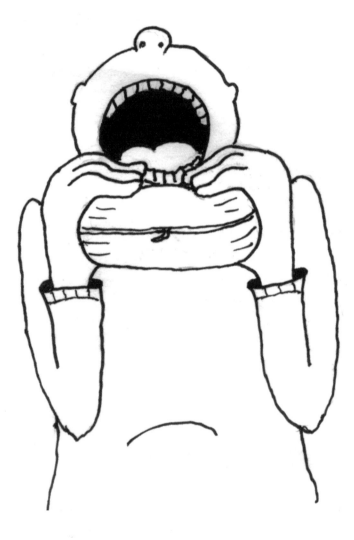

Toenail Teacake

I was cutting my toenails in the kitchen
When a nail flew up in the air.
I tried to find where it had landed
But I couldn't find it anywhere.

It had set off like a space rocket
Launched from nail cutter,
Shot across the room
And landed in the butter.

It wasn't until Dad toasted a teacake,
Took a bite and shouted, "Good grief!"
That I finally found my toenail:
It was stuck between Dad's teeth!

The Fat Fairy

Freda was a wood-fairy
Whose diet wasn't very good,
So she decided to leave her home
By the toadstools in Fairy Wood.

Someone who is two inches high
Shouldn't weigh over a pound;
She couldn't sit on a toadstool
Because she'd squash it to the ground.

Her fairy wings were useless;
She would flap them really hard
But fairy wings weren't designed
To lift a tub of lard.

So Freda had to walk,
Which caused her feet to ache,
Then she'd sit beneath a tree stump
And pig out on fairy cake.

This fairy was so miserable,
She would never find a mate,
And the more upset that she became
The more that Freda ate.

But things would soon change:
As she went to eat a bun
She accidentally dropped it down a hill
And boy, after it she did run!

She chased it down the hill
And over a little stream,
She ran so hard and swam so fast
That her ears were belching steam.

As the bun swept over a waterfall
Freda followed it with a splat,
Then watched in horror
As the bun was snatched by a rat.

Freda screamed, "Give me back my bun!"
As she swam to the waterside,
But the sight of a big, fat, wet fairy
Made the rat want to run and hide.

But Freda wasn't going to let it get away
So after the rat she started to run;
She would chase it day and night -
No rat was going to nick *her* bun!

And so she chased that rat
Until she collapsed upon the floor.
It was no good, she had to give in,
She just couldn't go on any more.

But Freda had done so much exercise
Trying to catch up to the rat
That now she was light and skinny
As she'd burnt off all her fat.

Freda joined the other fairies again,
No more crying for hours and hours.
When humans walked through the wood
She could now hide behind the flowers.

The next day Freda was so happy,
Although her muscles ached,
That she sat on a toadstool and ate a bun
From a tray of twelve that she'd baked!

Pete's Feet

There was once a young boy called Pete
Who had very, very stinky feet.
When he took off his shoes
It made the evening news
Because they had to evacuate his street.

A Pain in the Bum!

Miss Lewis once sat on a pin
That someone had put on her chair.
She screamed like a banshee
And jumped six feet in the air.

She ran around the class like a turkey,
It really was good fun
Watching her trying not to swear
While pulling the pin from her bum.

She said when she found out who did it
There would be such a price to pay,
And because of the pain in her bum
She couldn't sit down all day.

The One Minute Mile

Once, out in deepest Africa,
A man ran one mile in a minute
And everyone wanted to know
Just how the heck he did it.

They said to move so fast
His muscles must be like iron.
The man replied, "A mile in a minute's easy
When you're being chased by a lion!"

Bogey Full of Goodness

I don't think things can be good for you
Once they have been up your nose;
My brother says his bogies are
And he eats loads of those.

Don't Want to Bee?

I just don't want to be
A hedgehog, pheasant or toad
Because they end their days
Squashed on the road.

I just don't want to be
A wasp, bee or fly;
Being smacked with a paper
Is a sad way to die.

So what would I like to be?
Well, I just want to be me.

Chard

There was a young boy from Chard
Who thought he was really hard.
He would pick a fight
With anyone in sight
And from every school he was barred.

Bravefart

When the English invaded Scotland
For the Scots things looked really bad,
But the English would be soon beaten
By Wally Willis, a brave wee Scots lad.

He handed gas-masks to all his kinsmen
As the English charged at full tilt,
Then Wally bent down, turned around
And lifted up his kilt.

As the Scots put on the gas-masks
They thought they would be torn apart,
But Wally screamed, "Come on, you Sassenachs!"
Then let loose an almighty fart.

The fart sent out such shockwaves
That the whole English front line fell,
Before wiping out two thousand cavalry
With its terrible, evil smell.

The English started to retreat
And the Scottish took them to task,
But you couldn't find one Scotsman
Who would dare take off his gas-mask.

So the Scottish beat the English
And wee Wally Willis had played his part.
He has now gone down in Scottish history
As the boy known as Bravefart!

The Big Fight

Fight! Fight! Fight!
Ronnie and Darren are having a fight,
Ronnie will win,
He says he is right.
Darren says he'll punch out his lights.

Fight! Fight! Fight!
It all started this morning
When they were having their break,
Darren drank Ronnie's drink,
He said it was just a mistake.

Fight! Fight! Fight!
Darren threw the first punch
But Ronnie hit back,
Then the headteacher appeared
And gave them both the sack.

Fight! Fight! Fight!
It's wrong for two teachers to fight
Like a couple of young yobs.
Now, because of their stupid behaviour,
They're both looking for new jobs.

Cheap Jim-Jams

Every night when I try to sleep
In my pyjamas that were so cheap
As I turn, in the dark of night,
The static lights up my room so bright.
If my Mum would spend a little more cash
I'd wear pyjamas that didn't give me a rash.

Itchy Bum

One night in bed
My bum started twitching,
I tried to scratch it
But I could not stop it itching

So I woke up my Dad
And said, "I've got an itchy bum."
He replied, "At three in the morning
Go tell your problems to your Mum."

So I woke up my Mum
And said, "Something's not right."
She looked at my bum,
Which wasn't a pretty sight.

Mum said, "I've told you before,
Fingernails are full of germs,
But you wouldn't stop biting them
So now you have worms."

How could this have happened?
I was in such a state;
Mum had just told me
My bum had fishing bait!

I was in such shock
I could not make a sound;
Worms don't belong up your bum,
Worms belong in the ground!

The next day we got up at six,
The chemist opens early on Mondays.
My bum now felt so sore
I put an ice cube down my undies.

My Mum bought me some powder
And my bum's stopped twitching;
Now I can sleep at night
Because my bum's no longer itching.

If you can get worms up your bum
What next: slugs or snails?
I'm not taking any chances -
I've stopped biting my nails.

Bath Time Wrinkles

My hands develop wrinkles in the bath,
I don't know why they appear,
But they're not as bad as Grandma's -
She must have been in the bath for a year!

More than You Can Chew

A man was in the sea
And it was getting dark;
He didn't know below him
Swam a dirty great big shark.

The shark swam to eat him
But then it turned and flew,
You see the man was in the sea
Because he needed to use the loo!

Tights Spot of Trouble

There was once a bank robber called Fred,
Who was very stupid, it was said.
The police were soon on his case
Because they had seen his face -
He'd put the tights on his legs not his head!

No Bill Will

There was once a young man called Will,
Who would go to restaurants and eat his fill.
But he is now banned
From all the restaurants in the land
Because he would never ever pay the bill.

Pop Idol

Dad wanted to be a pop idol
And every night when he is dreaming
He can see himself singing songs,
While thousands of girls are screaming.

Mum says that he has achieved his dream,
He's just a different kind of idol.
She said, "Just look at him asleep on the couch,
You know that your pop is idle."

The Little Giant

If you walk in the land of giants
You do so at your peril,
Unless you meet a little girl
Who goes by the name of Beryl.

Beryl was such a lovely girl,
The apple of her father's eye.
Her parents were twenty feet tall,
But Beryl was only three feet high.

So they took her to the giant doctor
Who looked puzzled and shook his head.
"I've never seen anything like it,
She should be ten feet tall," he said.

The doctor asked Beryl questions,
Then he started to laugh.
He asked, "Do you have the water hot
When you have a bath?"

Beryl replied, "Yes, I love hot water,
It makes my skin so pink."
The doctor said, "Do you know a boil wash
Causes everything to shrink?"

So now Beryl has cool baths.
If you met her your toes would curl
Because now she's ten feet tall,
Yes, Beryl is one big girl!

The Cross Machine

A scientist invented a machine
That crossed things in the right mode,
So he crossed a sheep with a secret message
And he got a baa code!

Grandad Eats Bogies

Does your Grandad play tricks on you
Like my Grandad plays tricks on me?
He once told me he was eating a bogey
Which turned out to be a pea.

Everything he does is so gross.
He fries smelly blue cheese in a wok:
The smell is so bad it makes me sick
And he says the cheese is from his sock.

He does everything from picking his nose
To farting while eating his dinner.
He can burp the tune of *Yellow Submarine*
And says, "As a party trick that's a winner."

Todd and Rod

There once was a boy called Todd,
Who had a good friend called Rod.
They would walk through the sands
Holding each other's hands -
I always thought that they were odd.

Bonny Ronnie

There was once a young boy called Ronnie,
Whose girlfriend thought him quite bonny
So he was totally stumped
When she told him, "You're dumped!"
Then went out with a boy called Donny.

T.V.

T.V. spewing out radiation,
Frying the brains of a gullible nation.
Twenty four hours beamed into your room,
Don't go to the toilet they'll be back soon.

To a whole nation it's not apparent
That they worship celebrities without any talent.
Turn it off before your eyes start blotching.
Hundreds of channels and nothing worth watching.

Read, go out, listen to music that rocks -
Don't stay at home and stare at a box.

Green Hair Monster

Mum's friend dyed Mum's hair
The strangest colour I've ever seen.
She said it was ash blonde
But it turned out bright green.

My Dad started to laugh
And said that he would sort it out.
He said, "Hold these cabbage leaves,
Now you can pass as a Brussels sprout."

The Phoenix

The phoenix was a mythical bird
That could never be burned;
It rose out of a fire
And lots of fame it earned.

But it's not as good as a chicken,
No matter how good it looked
Because you could never eat it,
There's no way it could be cooked.

Trolley Folly

When we go to the supermarket
My Mum is just looking for a deal,
But when she picks a trolley
Why does it always have a wonky wheel?

No matter how I try to push it
It always veers off to the side,
Crashing into people's legs
As across the floor I glide.

I shout to people, "Coming through!"
Then one wheel will wedge
Sending me spinning across the floor
And dumping me in the veg.

There is an answer to this problem,
It seems so clear to me:
Each and every shopping trolley
Should have an M.O.T.

A Bet Too Far

There was once a gambler called Jude,
Who thought he was a dude.
In a gambling shack
He lost the clothes off his back
And had to walk home in the nude.

Growing Up

When Jason grows up he wants to be a fireman,
When John grows up he wants to drive a digger,
When Jane grows up she wants to be a teacher,
When I grow up I just want to be bigger!

Dead Fat

Here lies the body
Of Mr Peter Bread
Who ate too much
And now he's dead.

He ate grease
By the slab
With his loving wife,
Donna Kebab.

He now roams
As a ghost,
He doesn't float
As he's fatter than most.

Peter was due
To go to heaven
But the elevator cloud
Only reached floor seven.

To whichever god
At night you pray,
Ask to be kept safe
And out of the takeaway.

Come and Buy my Thingumyjig

Come and buy my thingumyjig,
It's not too small and not too big.
I will guarantee, if you try it,
You will certainly want to buy it.

Come on and buy my thingumyjig

When you're out, walking in town,
There'll be people marching up and down
With their clipboards in their hands,
Hunting you out, in their bands.

They want you to buy my thingumyjig

On an evening when you eat your dinner
We'll phone your Dad, tell him he's a winner.
We'll phone him from our call centre
To say he's won a competition he did not enter.

Everyone's a winner with my thingumyjig

Always remember that if it sounds funny
It usually is; they want your money.
You don't have to be in it to win it
And there's a mug born every minute.

So come on and buy my thingumyjig!

Get Your Teeth into School

It's no secret that I hate school,
No one hates school more than me,
But please, Mum, send me to school,
Today school is where I want to be.

Please, Mum, send me to school!
Forget all the bad things I've said.
Please don't take me to the dentist,
Send me to school instead.

Babbage

There was a young man called Babbage,
Whose farts were really quite savage.
When his wind would break
It could cause an earthquake
And left a terrible smell of cabbage.

The Earwax Candle

To make an earwax candle
Would be really quite absurd,
But if you lit an earwax candle
Would it repeat everything you've heard?

Lumpy Milk

Kirsty was thirsty so she raided the fridge
For something cold to drink.
From a milk bottle she drunk,
Swallowed a chunk
And her face turned a strange shade of pink.

She started to cough as the milk was off
And sour and lumpy and thick.
The milk then churned
As her stomach turned
And Kirsty wanted to be sick.

So if at night you are thirsty,
Please don't be like Kirsty.
Check whatever you drink;
If it's liquid so thick that it makes you feel sick
Please don't throw up in the sink.

Half Past Three

For five days a week
At half past three
Something so magical
Happens to me.
I feel so happy,
I laugh and shout,
And my friends and me
Start to mess about.
For five days a week
At half past three
A bell always rings
Then school ends for me.

Holiday Pain

Every year when we go on holiday
It is always the same,
The moaning will start
As soon as we get on the plane.

Are we there yet?
I want a wee.
Are we there yet?
I can't see the sea.
Are we there yet?
The weather looks glum.
Are we there yet?
My bum's gone numb.

Mum says she is fed up,
The moaning is driving her mad;
My sis and me don't moan,
The person who moans is my Dad!

Twickers Snickers

There was once a woman from Twickers
Who wore seriously large knickers.
One day as she spoke
Her knicker elastic broke
Because she'd pigged out on Snickers.

Meat Treat

I have chosen to be a vegetarian,
I won't eat meat for any price.
But I do have a problem:
I think bacon sandwiches smell so nice.

Home Alone

Mum, when you go out tonight
Please can I stay at home?
Don't send me to Auntie Bev's,
I want to be alone.

I won't answer the door to strangers,
I'll put on the door chain and latches.
I won't try to use the oven
And I promise not to play with matches.

All my friends stay home alone,
They do it all the time.
Please, please, trust me just once -
After all, I am forty-nine!

The Misunderstanding

My girlfriend has finished with me,
She has really broken my heart.
It was just a misunderstanding
Over a stupid great fart.

It wasn't even me who did it,
It was my dog, he's not well.
But I blamed my girlfriend
For making that terrible smell.

She stormed off saying,
"You think that you're smart,
But everyone knows
That girls never fart!"

My Old Man

Mum said she had an antique,
She said it's old and sad
But she could never sell it
Because her antique's my Dad.

No Bath Cath

There was once a young girl called Cath
Who had never had a bath.
When she passed by you could tell
Because of the terrible smell
That knocked out all in her path.

Can't Bear It!

If you go into the woods today
You will not believe your eyes;
All the bears are oh, so fat
Because they've eaten all the pies.

They're so big they cannot move,
Babies just lay there with their Mums
Spending their time farting and burping
And occasionally scratching their bums.

So who is to blame for this problem?
Who has been stupid and unwise?
Is it the people who feed the bears?
Or the bears for eating the pies?

Lonely Teachers

Teachers can never fall in love,
They never have good laughs
Because all that teachers think about
Is English, geography and maths.

Ealing Feeling

There was once a young man from Ealing,
In his stomach he had a funny feeling.
He ate baked beans one night
Then gave himself a fright
When his fart pebble-dashed the ceiling.

A Quiet Drink?

My little brother is crazy,
He's usually as quiet as a mouse
But if he drinks orangeade
He smashes up the house.

Old Man Clive

Once an old man called Clive,
Whose age was one hundred-and-five,
Was asked after such a long life
Would he like to have another wife.
He replied, "No, I'm just glad to be alive."

Tightwad Dad

My dad is so mean,
He's one of life's complainers.
He won't part with a hundred quid
To buy me a pair of trainers!

Piece of Pizza

There was a young man from Chiswick
Who would gobble up pizzas real quick.
He loved quattro stagioni
And spicy pepperoni
But anchovies made him feel sick.

The Magnificent Evan

This is one heck of a story,
One of those very strange tales:
It's about the green valleys
In a country called Wales.

The valleys were over-run
With bandits and sneaks
Who would raid the allotments
And steal all the leeks.

The gardeners wanted justice.
The mayor said, "I know of a man!"
So he put out a call
To the one known as Little Evan.

Now Evan was just three feet high
With muscles as hard as rocks.
He might not be very tall
But Evan was built like an ox.

He'd never met his real parents,
As a boy he was so lonely.
A miner had adopted him
To replace his dead pit pony.

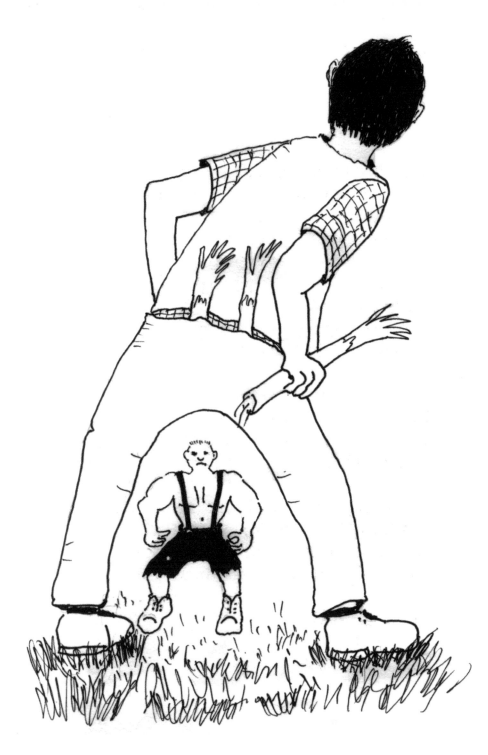

Evan dressed in old trousers,
On his chest no shirt, just braces.
On his feet were hob-nailed boots
That he wore without any laces.

This man was so tough
His body was as hard as iron,
And when faced with injustice
He would fight like a lion.

So on that fateful night,
Of which everyone still speaks,
Evan caught up with the bandits
Nicking Mr Jones's leeks.

He screamed, "Put down those leeks!"
The bandits gave him evil looks.
He was outnumbered twenty-to-one;
Things didn't look good for the crooks.

The bandits foolishly attacked
Which was a total disaster:
Half of them lost their teeth,
The rest ended up in plaster.

That night a message was sent
To every would-be thief:
Keep away from the leeks
Or you will lose your teeth.

The gardeners threw a party,
Everyone was having fun
But Evan walked away
Saying, "My work here is done."

So when the valleys are in trouble
They know there's a man
Who will come to their rescue:
He's called The Magnificent Evan.

Not the End of Love

After a long illness,
And early last week,
My mother died -
I can hardly speak.

The news of her death
Cut me like a knife;
It's broken my heart
And left a hole in my life.

My Dad can't cope,
He never sleeps.
He cuddles her photo
And sits and weeps.

I feel really angry,
I don't know why.
Then I feel guilty
Because I don't cry.

Grandma is brilliant,
She's always so strong
Saying, "When you're grieving
There's no right way or wrong."

Some people say a prayer,
If that's what they believe.
Others want to talk
To help them grieve.

Healing takes time;
I feel torn apart.
I will always love you, Mum,
With all of my heart.

For my wife, Carol

Acknowledgements

Thanks to The King's England three: Dopey, Bashful and Grumpy. Also, I would like to thank all the pupils, teachers, librarians and anyone else I've met on my travels for making me feel welcome.

I would also like to thank in advance any teachers/librarians who live in warm, foreign climes surrounded by sun, sea, and, most importantly, bars. Thank you for looking at the back of this book, seeing the telephone number and thinking, "I'll phone and book him to come over for a visit."